3

Built in USA: Post-war Architecture

FRANK LLOYD WRIGHT

Laboratory Tower for the Johnson Wax Company. Racine, Wisconsin. 1949

Photograph by Ezra Stoller

Built in USA: Post-war Architecture

EDITED BY

HENRY-RUSSELL HITCHCOCK AND ARTHUR DREXLER

The Museum of Modern Art

Distributed by Simon & Schuster New York

DEPARTMENT OF ARCHITECTURE AND DESIGN

Philip C. Johnson, *Director*
Arthur Drexler, *Curator*
Mildred Constantine, *Associate Curator of Graphic Design*
Greta Daniel, *Assistant Curator*
Georgette Methot, *Secretary*

Published by the Museum of Modern Art, 11 West 53rd Street, New York.
All rights reserved. Printed in England.

ADVISORY COMMITTEE:

Peter Blake, Associate Editor, *The Magazine of Building;*
Thomas H. Creighton, Editor, *Progressive Architecture;* John
D. Entenza, Editor, *Arts and Architecture;* Talbot F. Hamlin,
School of Architecture, Columbia University; Douglas Has-
kell, Architectural Editor, *The Magazine of Building;* Joseph
Hudnut, Dean, Graduate School of Design, Harvard Univer-
sity; Elizabeth Mock Kassler, writer and critic; Frank G.
Lopez, Senior Associate Editor, *Architectural Record;* Joseph
B. Mason, Executive Editor, *Architectural Record;* Charles
Magruder, Managing Editor, *Progressive Architecture;* G.
Holmes Perkins, Dean, School of Fine Arts, University of
Pennsylvania; P. I. Prentice, Editor and Publisher, *The Maga-
zine of Building.*

The Museum wishes to thank, in addition to the members of
the Advisory Committee, the following individuals for their
generous assistance: Ernest Farmer, Wilder Green, George
Howe, John MacL. Johansen, Edgar Kaufmann, Jr., John
Peter.

Book designed by Alvin Lustig

Contents

FRONTISPIECE Frank Lloyd Wright; Laboratory, Johnson Wax Company

5 ACKNOWLEDGEMENTS

8 PREFACE Philip C. Johnson

10 INTRODUCTION Henry-Russell Hitchcock

20 POST-WAR ARCHITECTURE Arthur Drexler

38 AALTO, ALVAR Senior Dormitory

40 AECK, RICHARD L. AND ASSOCIATES Stadium

42 AIN, GREGORY John Wilfong house

44 BARNES, EDWARD LARRABEE Ted Weiner house

46 BARTHELME, DONALD AND ASSOCIATES West Columbia Elementary School

48 BELLUSCHI, PIETRO Equitable Savings and Loan Association Building

50 BREUER, MARCEL Vassar Cooperative Dormitory

52 BREUER, MARCEL Harry A. Caesar house

54 CORBETT, MARIO Moritz Thomsen house

56 DAILEY, GARDNER A. AND ASSOCIATES Red Cross Building

58 EAMES, CHARLES Case Study House

60 FERGUSON, THE H. K., COMPANY Bluebonnet Plant

62 GROPIUS, WALTER, AND T. A. C. Harvard Graduate Center

64 HARRIS, HARWELL HAMILTON Ralph Johnson house

66 HARRISON AND ABRAMOVITZ Alcoa Building

68 HARRISON, WALLACE K., AND CONSULTANTS United Nations Secretariat

70 JOHANSEN, JOHN MACL. John MacL. Johansen house

72 JOHNSON, PHILIP C. Philip C. Johnson house

74 JOHNSON, PHILIP C. Richard Hodgson house

76 KENNEDY, KOCH, DE MARS, RAPSON AND BROWN Eastgate Apartments

78 KUMP, ERNEST J. San Jose High School

80 LYNDON, MAYNARD Vista Elementary School

82 MENDELSOHN, ERIC Maimonides Health Center

84 MIES VAN DER ROHE, LUDWIG Dr. Edith Farnsworth house

86 MIES VAN DER ROHE, LUDWIG Lake Shore Drive Apartments

88 MIES VAN DER ROHE, LUDWIG Boiler Plant

90 NEUTRA, RICHARD J. Warren Tremaine house

92 POLEVITSKY, IGOR Michael Heller house

94 SAARINEN, SAARINEN AND ASSOCIATES General Motors Technical Center

98 SAARINEN, SWANSON AND SAARINEN Opera Shed

100 SCHWEIKHER AND ELTING Louis C. Upton house

102 SKIDMORE, OWINGS AND MERRILL Lever House

104 SKIDMORE, OWINGS AND MERRILL Garden Apartments

106 SOLERI, PAOLO, AND MARK MILLS desert house

108 SORIANO, RAPHAEL Case Study House

110 TWITCHELL, RALPH S., AND PAUL RUDOLPH Albert Siegrist house

112 TWITCHELL, RALPH S., AND PAUL RUDOLPH W. R. Healy house

114 WRIGHT, FRANK LLOYD Johnson Wax Company Laboratory

118 WRIGHT, FRANK LLOYD V. C. Morris store

120 WRIGHT, FRANK LLOYD Herbert Jacobs house

122 WRIGHT, FRANK LLOYD Sol Friedman house

124 WRIGHT, LLOYD Wayfarers' Chapel

126 YEON, JOHN Visitors' Information Center

Preface PHILIP C. JOHNSON

The battle of modern architecture has long been won. Twenty years ago the Museum was in the thick of the fight, but now our exhibitions and catalogues take part in that unending campaign described by Alfred Barr as "simply the continuous, conscientious, resolute distinction of quality from mediocrity—the discovery and proclamation of excellence"

To make this "proclamation" from time to time is the prime function of the Department of Architecture and Design. This book is the second of its kind; the first, "Built in U.S.A. 1932–1944", summed up the work prior to World War II. This treats with the great post-war flowering of architecture in this country —which is so obvious around us.

The method of selecting buildings to be included in this exhibition and book is new in the Department's work. In order to make the final selections as representative as possible of current expert opinion the Museum appointed an Advisory Committee, which, without holding special meetings, have informally and by letter expressed their individual opinions and choices for inclusion and exclusion. However, to avoid the compromises to which committees in general are prone, and to sharpen the specific flavor of the selection, we felt that the final responsibility of choice should rest with one judge.

For that judge we chose Professor Henry-Russell Hitchcock of Smith College, the leading historian of modern architecture in this country. With me, Mr. Hitchcock was responsible for our first international exhibition of modern architecture exactly twenty years ago; and his association with the Museum has continued informally ever since. For the choices in this present book, however, Mr. Hitchcock, this time, has sole and complete responsibility.

The text of this book is divided into two sections. Henry-Russell Hitchcock addresses himself to the state of architecture in the United States today; Arthur Drexler, the Curator of the Department of Architecture and Design, discusses the buildings in this exhibition in particular.

The criterion of selection which Mr. Hitchcock has employed is a double one; in his own words: "quality and significance of the moment". This distinction is important to understand. There are buildings included which are pertinent more because of their significance in the story of architecture than for their quality, and conversely, there are buildings of quality—say by Mies or Wright—which are omitted since more significant buildings of these two architects have been included. In a greater or less degree, however, every building does satisfy both criteria.

It has not been our intention to include *all* buildings of quality or significance. The book, as Henry-Russell Hitchcock complains, is much too small—so great is the quantity of good building in these post-war years. Also some good buildings may have been omitted because they were completed too late for inclusion at the time of our June 1952 deadline. We hope in these cases to include them in later exhibitions.

It is certain that no committee member would agree with all of Mr. Hitchcock's selections—I certainly cannot myself—but no two individuals can always agree. On the other hand everyone cannot help but agree that the buildings included show a startling development compared with the material of the 1944 exhibition; and if we should think back twenty years to the 1932 exhibition the change is more striking. The International Style which Henry-Russell Hitchcock's book of 1932 heralded has ripened, spread and been absorbed by the wide stream of historical progress. Every building in this book would look different if it had not been for the International Style, yet few buildings today recall the rigorous patterns of those days— the cubic boxes with asymmetric window arrangements so characteristic of the twenties.

With the mid-century modern architecture has come of age.

Introduction HENRY-RUSSELL HITCHCOCK

H. H. Richardson,
Marshall Field Store. 1887

By the middle of the twentieth century, American architecture has come to occupy a position of special prominence in the world, such as had been promised ever since the appearance of Henry Hobson Richardson as a great master some seventy-five years ago. Towards this prominence two things have particularly contributed: on the one hand the very considerable production of a controlled economic boom, and on the other the continuing activity of various architects belonging to several successive generations whose abilities are fully worthy of their present opportunities. The fact that among these architects are several whose original reputations were made in Europe proves that American architecture is not an isolated phenomenon: in architecture, as in many other things, we are the heirs of Western civilization. Our own greatest master, Frank Lloyd Wright, now in his eighties more active than ever, is today not only honored throughout the world but also at home. We have also provided important commissions hardly obtainable today abroad for several distinguished Europeans who have settled in our midst or who have been invited to design or to advise on the design of major structures.

Booms are not always conducive to good building, and memories of excessive production in the twenties should warn us to view with a wary eye such construction as is prepared and executed under conditions of maniac haste and rising costs. In general, however, standards have been maintained this time and even lifted above those of the pre-war period. The purpose of this exhibition and book is to provide some definition of those standards and, in the midst of quantity production, to put critical emphasis firmly upon quality by exercising a rigid selectivity.

To select rigidly means to exclude much that is respectable and even distinguished—there are obviously many more than forty-three edifices built in the last few years worthy of admiration; to select primarily for quality, moreover, must necessarily give an inaccurate statistical picture of current building production. Certain areas of building are over-represented; others not represented at all. In the first "Built in U.S.A." exhibition in 1944, which followed twelve years after the Museum's first architectural exhibition, the emphasis was rather upon the extent of the contribution of modern architects. In those important years of early acceptance and rapid spread of the ideas that had seemed so novel in the exhibition of 1932, too rigid standards in selection would have defeated the purpose of the project.

Today there is no further need to underline the obvious fact that what used to be called "traditional" architecture is dead if not buried. It may be categorically stated—and requires no illustrations to make such a statement plausible—that there is today no realm of building in which respectable modern work is not being done.

Sociological criteria might have demanded the inclusion of certain categories of construction—notably public housing—in which at the present time quality is conspicuously low. Regional tactfulness, so to say, might have suggested, particularly as regards private houses, the inclusion of examples from more parts of the country than are here represented. But such considerations would defeat the purpose of the book and the exhibition, which is to show the best that is being built as far as that may be done within a very limited compass. Chronological considerations have provided no absolute guidance, but the war and immediate post-war conditions of the years 1944–48 were not as conducive to satisfactory architectural production, for many reasons both economic and psychological, as the last five years have been.

Architects have not been represented on reputation alone: that is to say that for one reason or another many architects of recognized distinction from coast to coast, authors of earlier work of very high quality, have not in this particular period produced buildings of especial interest. There have, however, been two slightly opposed considerations in the choice of the architects represented, as distinguished from the choice of individual works. The selection definitely leans toward the inclusion of new men who have come on the scene only in this post-war period. After a first fine flare, some of these post-war careers may well fizzle out; but with young men who may as yet have but one or two modest works to their credit this exhibition has seemed a proper place to underline their promise. On the other hand, the greatest masters, Wright and Mies van der Rohe, are perhaps over-represented, since all their production tends to be on a level to which others attain only very occasionally.

Among the architects from abroad Le Corbusier can only be represented through his contribution toward the design of the United Nations Secretariat since no American client has yet seen fit to employ him to build here. It is worth noting that it is his *Unité d'Habitation* in Marseille, rather than the United Nations Secretariat, that maintains his rank as an equal of the great masters practicing in this country. Aalto's and Mendelsohn's buildings in this country stand rather higher in the total roster of their production than does Gropius' Harvard Graduate Center (in any event technically the work of The Architects' Collaborative). Only of Mies, among the later arrivals from abroad, can it be asserted that he has built here work as fine as that on which his earlier reputation was based. And that assertion might not stand were his Barcelona Pavilion of 1929 still extant. Eero Saarinen represents with distinction the second generation of famous architects in his family. His work is American always; his father's to the last remained somewhat Finnish. Neutra and Belluschi, despite their foreign origin, may be considered, like Saarinen, wholly American. This is also true of Gropius' former partner, Marcel Breuer, to whom some of the credit must go for a good deal of Gropius' early work in this country.

Climates, both physical and psychological, have long differentiated American regions. But regional stylisms in architecture are in fact relatively undifferentiated; the ablest architects, like Wright from his earliest days, know how to be successful regionalists of all the regions they are called upon to work in. One may properly speak of a Boston or of a Bay Region *group* of architects, each group having certain aesthetic purposes as well as characteristic practical problems in common. But in many ways, considering—as compared to European countries—the enormous distances between one region and another and their disparate climates and available building materials—it is the homogeneity of American production that is surprising.

Modern architectural design in America is today more nationally standardized—in a good sense—than is the building

Le Corbusier, Apartment house, Marseille. 1952

Ludwig Mies van der Rohe,
German Pavilion, Barcelona Exposition.
1929

industry. The major influences are national and ideas pass rapidly from one area to another. Even the two California regions have far more in common with other parts of the country than it is generally supposed.

But modern architecture is not—as some have hoped and others feared—monolithic. Names that have already been mentioned here—Wright, Gropius, Mies van der Rohe, Mendelsohn, Aalto, to recall only the better known—provide sufficient evidence that various directions, not necessarily opposed but certainly not strictly parallel, are represented in production of distinction. Most of these directions have been set by older men, but in all cases there are younger representatives moving the same way with skill and with a quite personal flair. Twenty years ago, when the first exhibition of modern architecture was held at the Museum, Wright's work seemed so differently conceived from that of the Europeans who had come on the architectural scene in the twenties that it could be considered passé. Since then, however, Wright has had an enormous resurgence of vital activity; his international reputation and critical influence has not been higher in forty years. To use the crude terms favored in partisan argument, the "functional" has not superseded the "organic" (nor for that matter is the reverse occurring in the way certain foreign admirers of Wright would like to claim). At one time an "international" mode in architecture seemed alien to Americans because its chief illustrations were to be seen only in Europe; to many Europeans today the same mode seems to epitomize what they most admire—or, as the case may be, most dislike in America. The largest examples of current building in continuation of the European mode of the twenties are by American firms such as Harrison and Abramovitz or Skidmore, Owings and Merrill; the influence of Gropius and of Mies van der Rohe, radiates from America as strongly as it ever did from Germany.

In America as elsewhere one cannot help noting the slower pace of architectural development compared to that of twenty-five or thirty years ago. We are now well into the post-war years, but neither in theory nor in practice have there been proposed such revolutions as made the 1920's so exciting. There has been a reaction, notably before and during the war, in Switzerland and the Scandinavian countries: a new "Empiricism" or a new "cosiness"; but there has now come a reaction against that reaction. The "classic" works of the beginning of modern architecture, not only those of a quarter century ago but of the 1890's, seem more relevant today and in some curious sense more up to date than the feeble attempts of the late thirties and forties to break away from the path that Sullivan and Mackintosh and Horta and Loos set out upon two generations ago.

To attempt to characterize the alternative directions of current architectural design too concretely would be to suggest that mid-century production is still eclectic in a superficial sort of way; that clients consciously choose architects, like many represented in this selection of buildings, who are for example Miesian or Wrightian, if they are hesitant to approach those masters directly. But this is an exaggerated dichotomy. If there be a "school", it would be that of Gropius, whose leading position as an educator and whose discussion of theory in lectures and books provides a more coherent body of architectural doctrine than do Wright or the rather inarticulate Mies van der Rohe. But the actual work of the Gropiusites, so to call them, derives in fact more from the practice of his former pupil and partner Breuer than from his own. The doctrine whose usual results are most surely recognizable and which at present is probably most widespread is that which the interpreters of Mies van der Rohe's thought and practice have provided.

Architects generally, both the young and the middle-aged, are less hide-bound than they once were. The old firms that remain in practice from the beginning of the century or from the twenties are now ready to provide their clients with what are supposed to be "modern" buildings, and the results of their subservience to a successful stylistic revolution are not as inferior as might be expected. Even in the more doctrinaire camps there is less tendency to see heresy on all sides or to claim that architectural salvation lies only in particular sociological or technological approaches.

It is not as easy as it was eight years ago to define contemporary architectural development in terms of particular modes of planning or of structure. What applies to New York or Chicago skyscrapers may not apply at all to Florida or Connecticut houses. One may observe that there is an increased interest in the spatial envelope of buildings, which is an interest related to a greater preoccupation with groups of contiguous edifices; one may note that America is still laggard in concrete construction compared to the Latin countries; and one may

15

affirm that prefabrication, so long discussed, so much experimented with, has not yet had the success of, say, the Hertfordshire school-building methods in England.

Architectural ambition seems to have departed from the ranks of those architects who design large-scale public housing at just the point when Le Corbusier in France and younger men like Powell and Moyer in England (where little other building is permitted), have shown that a new and more vigorous sculptural expression can be as "functional" as our barrack-like blocks of the pre-war period, which have aged into visual slums almost before their mortar dried.

Industrial work remains on a high level comparatively and yet, as always, individual factories of particular distinction are hard to find. Schools almost everywhere are cleanly and freshly designed, yet rarely do they ever achieve much individual character. Large houses are built less and less; but smaller houses, for all their simplicity, are neither cheaper to erect nor, in their somewhat puritanical way, less luxurious. But such comments are more relevant when applied to the individual buildings illustrated, and any more particular statements which might be set down concerning materials or approaches to design would readily be contradicted by individual buildings included in the selection which follows.

Quality and significance of the moment, has been the criterion, and quality is in any period extraordinarily difficult to define since it depends more on the effectiveness of the individual solution than on the rigid application of this or that formula. The historical fact is that most periods have been more various in their building production than we find it convenient to remember. Even with hindsight we cannot always work out stylistic sequences in the glib way certain critics, on *a priori* grounds, would assume that the manner of Gropius necessarily succeeds that of Wright, who is some fifteen years his elder but who has never been more active and rarely so influential as he is today.

Modern architectural criticism has tended to eschew many terms favored in the immediately preceding generations because of the unhappy connotations such words have acquired. Beauty, character, grace, and elegance have found little favor as terms of praise with a generation seeking extra-aesthetic sanctions for an architectural revolution. It was easier and less committing to speak only of the functional effectiveness of certain plan solutions and the economy—real or hypothetical—

of certain structural systems. A generation sybaritic in many other ways was content to house its activities, as it were, in architectural blue jeans.

To boast of the high cost of anything—the first boast of the contemporary film producer—was for architects in the worst of taste. As building costs rose, architects prated only of economy, and it was assumed that a hypothetical business man's attitude of strict accountancy and budget paring was the only proper one for a serious professional practitioner. Yet actually it has been business, interested in the advertising value of striking architecture, which has sponsored many of the more luxurious—and not to balk at a word—beautiful buildings of the last few years. Lever Brothers in New York, General Motors in Detroit, the Johnson Wax Company in Racine have been among the more conspicuous Maecenases who have backed their architects in putting quality before economy. The extravagances of the twenties have not returned; no magnates

Frank Lloyd Wright, Robie house. 1909

Pier Luigi Nervi, Stadium, Florence.

1932

aim to have their architects produce the tallest buildings in the world; but even the brochures that seek funds for the erection of educational edifices emphasize, overtly or tacitly, the presumptive distinction of the architects chosen and of their designs. Architecture is not merely an aspect of the practical side of civilization; its functions are not merely material; and from the young couples straining their borrowing power to employ Wright, to the board of corporations and institutions seeking prestige through the employment of a Saarinen or a Louis Kahn, this is now much more readily recognized than it was only a few years ago. Architecture, in the prestige sense, once represented an outlay for imitative exteriors: industrial research laboratories were built with Doric columns, as well as college libraries with Tudor or Georgian detail. But today, when money is spent to obtain prestige through visual effect, it is more likely to go into essentials—more space around the buildings and better organized landscape settings; materials that are intrinsically attractive as well as serviceable in the practical sense; and finally on interior space, that basic architectural commodity which once cost little or nothing and which today is dearer than marble walls or gold-plated plumbing.

To write of current American architecture while the tawdry results of the boom of the twenties clog our cities cannot but induce a certain present complacency. One must think back a little further to realize what real sacrifices modern architecture has made in variety, in detailed expressiveness and even in certain psychological aspects of comfort—in privacy for example and in separate spatial provision for separate living functions. If elderly architects, men in their sixties and their eighties, retain so much prestige in a world otherwise dedicated to youth, it is partly because they have carried through from the earlier climate of the period before World War I a strong faith in the cultural value of architecture. Dedicated, their lights still shine for the youngest generation, while the sociological lights of the middle generation have now burned somewhat dim. Not so long ago certain thinkers liked to see the problems of building as something each generation might solve *de novo* for itself, tearing down all that was inherited and erecting everything anew to last a few decades before it in turn was replaced. But the world's cities have remained full of structures fifty and a hundred years old. We are forced now to consider, as so few modern architects did in the twenties, how buildings will wear through a generation or more, and whether they are likely to grow obsolete visually even more rapidly than they must do physically.

Dedicated to change both as a people and as a generation, twentieth-century Americans have condoned the chaos of their cities and the low caliber of the buildings of which they are composed on the theory that they would soon get around to replacing and re-erecting everything from scratch. Great monuments of earlier days have been destroyed in order to provide parking places, while at the same time ill-planned new structures go up sending more traffic into the city streets. To build well—and that in the final analysis means to design well—may cost more at the start; but the building that lasts the longest, not merely in terms of practical satisfactions but of aesthetic satisfactions as well, will be cheaper in the long run. Structures must be at once solider and more elastic so that they may live out the years it takes to pay for them and still be capable of changes in functional use hardly to be foreseen. Once it was supposed skyscrapers would serve their generation and be replaced by better ones, and that houses would provide for one stage in a family's growth or decline and then be jettisoned when the family moved into a new stage. Today this cheerful innocence is rapidly passing, and that fact has redounded to the advantage of our mid-century architecture; we are, I think, grown somewhat more sober now.

Post-war Architecture ARTHUR DREXLER

Architecture, even before it is sound planning or adequate plumbing, is conspicuous space. The methods by which architects today habitually organize space to make it conspicuous are largely derived from the work of three men: Frank Lloyd Wright, Ludwig Mies van der Rohe, and Charles Le Corbusier. Their work has contributed to a common fund of ideas, and, as many of the buildings in this book suggest, their influence is acknowledged even by those architects who most readily depart from it.

That there should now be a grammar of architectural style is a possibility not everywhere regarded with enthusiasm. Wright himself, for example, invents new forms for each experience of space his buildings are designed to offer. His architecture is an exuberant elaboration—a three-dimensional commentary on a building's function or on its particular structural form. Thus each of Wright's buildings may have its own style.

But on the other hand Mies van der Rohe, excluding from his architecture whatever is not directly related to structure, makes structural clarity a value independent of the specific buildings that occasion it. He is thus able to assert the quality of his ideas even at those moments when buildings, as Paul Valéry says, should speak rather than sing: a boiler plant Mies designed for the Illinois Institute of Technology is distinguished architecture. Yet no building by Mies, in the United States, shows more clearly the relation between conspicuous space and the structure that generates it than does his house for Dr. Edith Farnsworth, in Illinois.

The Farnsworth house consists of three horizontal planes: a terrace, a floor, and a roof. Welded to the leading edge of each plane are steel columns which keep them all suspended in mid-air. Because they do not rest *on* the columns, but merely touch them in passing, these horizontal elements seem held to their supports by magnetism. Floor and roof appear as opaque planes defining the top and bottom of a volume whose sides are simply large panels of glass. The Farnsworth house is, indeed, a quantity of air caught between a floor and a roof.

To preserve the continuity of this space, interior partitions have been avoided as much as possible. Bathrooms, heating unit, a fireplace, and kitchen equipment are all collected in a large box set well to one side of the room. Varying quantities of space around this utility core become dining, lounge, and sleeping areas. The house must be thought of as a single room containing a box, and thus the utility core stops short of the ceiling, emphasizing its character as a house within a house.

The illusion of effortless organization is reinforced by the superb craftsmanship with which the building has been executed. For example, the ceiling is a paper-smooth expanse of plaster separated from the steel framing which holds the glass by a narrow indentation—a kind of incised, negative molding. The steel, painted white, was first sandblasted to achieve the desired precision of surface. Both the terrace and the house are paved with Italian travertine, and perhaps the most beautiful details of all are the handsomely proportioned travertine steps which lead first to the terrace, and from there to the house itself, with an easy, flowing generosity not often seen in modern architecture. Each detail and each material, including the champagne-colored raw silk curtains, is used to clarify an absolute—one could say a Platonic—architectural space, serenely independent of the transient emotional values of light, location, and atmosphere. But, in its cumulative effect, the Farnsworth house generates emotional overtones as insistent as the hum of a dynamo.

Ludwig Mies van der Rohe, page 84

The most formidable urban objects in the United States are Mies' twin glass and steel apartment towers on Chicago's Lake Shore Drive. If these buildings provoke the emotional response to urban life so well described by Franz Kafka, it is because 860 Lake Shore Drive is Metropolis defined, as Dr. Edith Farnsworth's pavilion is the House abstracted. At its most rewarding, Mies' architecture states a problem with the clarity of revelation, and these imposing glass boxes glittering on Chicago's strand are three-dimensional diagrams of the type multi-story vertical building. In this particular case they are dwellings. Essentially linear in design, the buildings are

Ludwig Mies van der Rohe, page 84

developed in shape and detail from the structural logic of a steel armature. Floor slabs, or rather ceilings, are always visible because the exterior walls are entirely of glass.

The apartments were originally planned with a minimum of interior partitions and with wood doors reaching to the ceiling (so that the walls appeared as unbroken planes). To meet the requirements of the owners the apartments were later given a more conventional layout, thus sacrificing something of the spaciousness desirable for rooms with outer walls completely open to the view. The interiors are not the buildings' most interesting feature, and an appraisal of 860 Lake Shore Drive, if it is to be relevant, should be concerned primarily with those abstractions of the building process which have preoccupied the architect.

Stretching from floor to floor, the glass walls become a gigantic mirror shimmering with reflections over most of its surface but with occasional transparent patches at the corners, through which one sees the sky. Regular in plan and twenty-six stories high, both towers are placed at oblique angles to the drive and at right angles to each other. Each tower is five bays long and three wide. The studied proportions of this basic grid are modified by the addition of vertical steel I-beams welded to the leading edge of each floor. This divides the bays into three parts and incidentally provides mullions for the window units. Seen head-on a facade appears like a mirror striped with railroad tracks. Seen at an angle the same facade looks like an enormous portière of narrow steel beams. The two buildings in conjunction, seen from almost any angle, present combinations of surface density ranging from a seemingly opaque massing of vertical steel beams to an open cage filmed over with glass.

In an architecture based on the logic of construction Mies has used structural elements primarily for a non-structural purpose. The importance of these steel *appliqués* is that they suggest a vocabulary of ornament inherent in the concept of the steel cage. Like those Gothic cathedrals—structural webs of stone filled with colored glass—which transcend the decoration of structure by becoming themselves pure decoration, Mies' decorative steel indicates a potential development of what is now the most refined style of our time.

No doubt architecture has had no client, for many years, as distractingly ennobling as the United Nations Organization. Directing a committee of architects recruited from all the member nations, Wallace Harrison has co-ordinated a stupefyingly complex program in a project of obvious, if controversial, monumentality.

The first of the United Nations buildings to be completed is the Secretariat tower. It is a thin slab rising directly from the ground for thirty-nine floors, terminated by a grille intended to conceal mechanical equipment on the roof. The extremely narrow end walls are surfaced with grayish-white marble; the two remaining facades, facing the East River and, towards the west, the jagged, arbitrary congeries of New York's skyscrapers, are entirely sheathed in green-tinted glass. It is these two facades, together with the building's extraordinarily slender proportions, that give the Secretariat its tremendous architectural impact.

In the character of so much post-war building, the glass facades absorb their surroundings and, in a way, merge with them. Reflections, once considered by Poussin, we are told, unworthy of serious art, are here no trivial embellishment; they are indeed the very point of the building. The Secretariat tower is an enormous vertical mirror in a white marble frame, set at the edge of a city stuffed like an arsenal with buildings never more appealing than when their chaos is converted by reflections to a casual and harmless decoration. In this sense the Secretariat tower depends for its effect in no small part on the contrast with its surroundings, which might with generosity be described as unfortunate.

Often criticized because it enshrines mere office workers in a monument dominating the more recognizably purposeful General Assembly Hall, the Secretariat tower is nevertheless a logical and convenient accommodation for the 3,400 office employees presently required by the United Nations. It was desirable to recognize that these employees *are*, in a practical sense, the machinery of the organization, even if one might prefer a more spiritualized symbol of constructive international accord. The heroic proportions of this accessory building thus derive naturally from the program. If the details which encumber the Secretariat tower served, instead, to clarify and reinforce its uncompromising, aggressively scaled geometry, the building's effect would have been as convincing at close range as it is from a distance.

For example, as a narrow vertical slab the building follows precedents well established by Le Corbusier, the great French architect who represented his country on the board of design consultants and whose concepts dominate the entire project.

Wallace K. Harrison and consultants,

page 68

But in his own more recent work, notably the huge apartment house in Marseille, Le Corbusier has shown the advantages of contrasting rounded sculptural forms on the roof (to house mechanical equipment) with the rectangularity of a slab building. In its use of a deceptive and awkward grille to conceal these units the Secretariat building seems to recapitulate the ideas Le Corbusier has himself discarded. But even as a recapitulation, the flat purity of form insisted upon with such good effect for the tower is marred by the corner detail joining the glass to the marble. Here the thin edge of the marble wall is cut back to make an extra molding around the glass. This inappropriate detail serves merely to blur the transition from glass to marble rather than to clarify it. But regardless of such blemishes the Secretariat tower is an impressive, even moving architectural experience. It is certainly one of the most dramatic and beautiful vertical buildings in the United States.

Lever House, the twenty-eight story office building on New York's Park Avenue for Lever Brothers' own use, combines a Miesian discipline of detail with a basic concept outlined thirty years ago by Le Corbusier. Having reduced the multi-story urban building to a glass-walled slab framed by solid end walls, he then lifted it clear of the ground so that parks and roads might run beneath. Lever House does not conform to all the stylistic proscriptions of Le Corbusier's early work, nor have its architects—Skidmore, Owings, and Merrill, with Gordon Bunschaft as chief designer—attempted a radical solution to urban planning problems. What they have attempted and achieved is a building which, simply in order to be seen, makes a great gift of air and light to the streets around it. The actual tower itself appears to begin three stories above the sidewalk. A glass-walled lobby and a small service area are the only enclosed spaces at street level, leaving the rest of the site unoccupied except for a pleasant bit of garden. Raised on columns sheathed in stainless steel, mid-way between the street and the apparent beginning of the tower, is a single floor of offices. This forms an arcade around the garden extending the full length and width of the site. There are no stores.

Air conditioning makes moveable windows for the tower unnecessary, and because they reach to the ceiling and continue in an unbroken ribbon around three sides of each floor, they offer a remarkable view of the city. They also produce a curious optical illusion: the observer seems to be in an airplane hovering directly above Park Avenue.

The tower is sheathed entirely in glass; glare and heat resistant green glass for the windows and a darker blue-green glass for the solid parapets. A web of thin stainless steel members weaves a plaid-like pattern across the facades. Some of these steel lines are mullions to hold the glass; others are tracks to guide a traveling gondola up, down, and across the facades as its passengers bathe the glass in soap-suds. A patron's rewards for being architecturally informed are seldom so gratuitous, but, like the building itself, this engaging animated advertisement for Lever Brothers' products may be commended to those of our giant corporations now aspiring to build well—an achievement of theirs to which we may all look forward.

Skidmore, Owings and Merrill, page 102

Eric Mendelsohn's Maimonides Health Center is a pleasantly urbane building set in an undistinguished part of San Francisco. Fourteen stories high, the main block is shielded from the street by a low entrance pavilion and by a gallery opening on a landscaped court. On the garden facade the floors are cantilevered beyond the columns (and framed by projecting end walls) so that each room opens on a continuous balcony—or more accurately on a wide promenade expanded at four points into semicircular balconies. At their maximum point of projection these concrete floor slabs are only three inches thick. The thin iron railings with which the balconies are equipped complete a lightly drawn, buoyant facade which, as one sees it from the entrance pavilion, seems peculiarly congenial to the building's program. It is true that the balconies are rather like embroidery on an otherwise stolid architectural cloth. But they are an engaging diversion of obvious utility, and it is a pity that the present directors of the Health Center, intent on increasing bed space, have had the balconies enclosed without obtaining from the architect the details appropriate to such a conversion, and which, in his hands, would have preserved the building's original interest and vitality.

The best of the recent skyscrapers use curtain walls, if not walls entirely of glass, in ways that demonstrate the ambiguity of the multi-story structural frame. Pietro Belluschi's office building for the Equitable Savings and Loan Association, in Portland, Oregon, is a concrete frame so tightly sheathed in aluminum and glass that no part projects more than seven-eighths of an inch, producing a dazzling but uniformly flush surface. The patches and lines of shadow which customarily give scale and emphasis have not been replaced by other detail, and the somewhat uneventful facades are a consequence of

25

expressing the structure as a cage whose members are in unstressed equilibrium. 860 Lake Shore Drive is clad in a vertical pin-stripe of steel, and Lever House and the United Nations Secretariat are hung with great glass curtains which tend to conceal the underlying structure rather than assign to it a specific directional character.

A fourth interpretation of the curtain wall—perhaps the most original that we have yet had—is that designed by Harrison and Abramovitz for the Alcoa building in Pittsburgh. Here the wall is composed of light screens of aluminum, $6' \times 12'$, with an almost square window punched through the center. Alcoa's window is literally a hole in the wall, equipped with a single pivoting panel of the ubiquitous green-tinted heat resistant glass. The aluminum sheets are only one-eighth of an inch thick. They are stamped in a pattern of triangular facets for greater rigidity, and after being attached to the framework (the crew working inside the building) the panels are sprayed with a four inch backing of perlite and sand.

Harrison and Abramovitz, page 66

Seen from the street Alcoa's evenly patterned, squarish, round-cornered windows look like several thousand television sets. The facets of the aluminum panels catch and break the light in triangular patches, lending to the facades a shifting diagonal movement and a sculptural interest reminiscent of, say, the rustications of the Czernin Palace.

If its surface richness makes the Alcoa building outstanding, the massing of the L-shaped tower, and much of its detail, contribute little. The interiors are without distinction; as in most office buildings a bow to significant space is made in the elevator landings with a veneer of some suitable stone (travertine); that is all. But, apart from its excellent and original facades, in one other aspect the building has a generosity comparable to Lever House. The lobby has been designed as a completely separate rectangular building four stories high, with its roof cantilevered from the aluminum-clad tower. This vertical space like the nave of a cathedral is entirely glass-enclosed, even on the side facing the main building a few feet away. The arrangement provides an entrance hall of resounding grandeur, with an element of fantasy appropriate to a glinting, faceted tower rising so abruptly out of the street.

But in respect of fantasy no building even approaches the marvellous concrete corkscrew Frank Lloyd Wright has planned for New York City's Museum of Non-Objective Art. It is intended for a corner site on upper Fifth Avenue, facing Central

Harrison and Abramovitz, page 66

Park, and it is hoped that construction will begin in the near future; this would be the first building in New York by the greatest of American architects. The building is a continuous spiral ramp, expanding as it rises into wider and wider circles. At the very top is a glass dome one hundred feet in diameter. Visitors to the Museum would take an elevator to the uppermost level and walk slowly down. The building is to be executed in reinforced concrete, and according to its architect it would, in the event of some aerially inflicted disaster, bounce like a spring but never collapse.

Wright's architecture has always been grounded in the emotional experience of space, light, and materials, and each of his buildings offers it with a resourcefulness that transcends

Frank Lloyd Wright, page 114

the merely imaginative. But even Wright himself has seldom produced a building that makes such uninhibited sport of technical virtuosity as his research laboratory tower for the Johnson Wax Company in Racine, Wisconsin. The first project executed by Wright for this wise client, in 1939, was the company's administration building—a hall four hundred feet long, with concrete columns terminating in flat discs, and arrayed like a squadron of golf tees, to support a roof of translucent glass tubes. Now Wright has added to the administration building a fourteen story tower set like a campanile in a walled courtyard of curiously Italian mood. The tower is connected to the main building by a covered walk lined with reflecting pools; here the light makes patterns on a roof modeled with cup-like indentations to form a series of small, inset domes.

The laboratory tower itself is built around a central shaft housing an elevator, stair, and mechanical equipment. From this shaft the floors are cantilevered like the numerous layers of an old-fashioned tier table. Each laboratory is two stories high. Its lower floor is square in plan, but rounded slightly at the corners, and its much smaller mezzanine floor is circular. By alternating these square and circular floor slabs Wright was able to sheathe the tower with horizontal glass tubes in expanses interrupted only once for every two floors, thus heightening the apparent scale of the building. The laboratories are flooded with light from these translucent glass walls, and, seen from the courtyard in full sunlight, their sparkling texture is most beautiful. But the building is seen at its best with sunlight behind it, so that the circular mezzanine floors appear through the glass in dim and shimmering silhouette.

One other major building of Wright's executed since the war offers spatial effects as astonishing as are the effects of light and texture in the Johnson tower. This is the store for V. C. Morris on San Francisco's Maiden Lane. Passers-by can avoid entering it only by a concentrated effort at indifference, so accurately has Wright calculated his sequence of surprises.

Frank Lloyd Wright, page 118

The facade is a blank wall of buff-colored brick, cut into at one side by a small arch. This opens to a tunnel with a very low vaulted roof, half brick and half glass; it is this glass section of the tunnel that serves as the store's "window", and its size and placement exactly control the angle at which the interior is first revealed. Looking diagonally up and across the space one sees the top of a ramp merging with the parapet of a circular gallery. The ceiling, suspended beneath a skylight, is made of

Frank Lloyd Wright, page 118

translucent plastic sheets and bubbles. A soft, sandy-surfaced plaster has been used for the ramp and its attendant walls; the floor is paved with stone. Glass, silver, and chinaware are displayed in walnut cabinets and shelves.

On entering the store one realizes that the great circular ramp almost fills the available space, or rather it shapes the space like an eggbeater stirring liquid in a bowl. The impact of the ramp's spiraling ascension into the light, abruptly terminated by the glowing, sculptural ceiling, can be said to humble the most aggressive customer. Certainly the Morris store introduces architecture to a kind of building usually without distinction in this country, and the response of the crowds who visit the store indicate that it is a welcome departure. The Morris store also gives us some hint of the effects Wright will obtain with the spiraling ramp and glass dome of his project for the Museum of Non-Objective Art.

Financially one of the most lavish undertakings of recent years is Eero Saarinen's Technical Center for General Motors. On a huge, perfectly flat site outside Detroit, Saarinen has assembled three buildings—many more are projected—around a rectangular pool the size of an athletic field. The low, long administration building is a frame of light steel members spaced five feet apart and filled with green-tinted glass. Seen in sharp perspective, as it must unless it is seen from a great distance, the repetitiousness of these vertical elements is exaggerated and suggests a facade turned out mechanically by the yard—an effect characteristic of many interpretations of Mies van der Rohe's architecture, and one which may be fundamentally suited to an architecture of increasingly industrial origin.

Saarinen, Saarinen and Associates, page 94

Solid panels on all the buildings in the group are of highly glazed, textured brick, prepared in a kiln built by General Motors on the site. The bricks are in tones of burnt orange and blue, very bright, and not a little unlike Persian faience ware. Most effective as counterpoint to the regularity of the structural systems employed, these bright rectangles of color, spotted like flags on the horizon, overcome the diffusion of architectural impact which results from the dispersal of buildings on a flat landscape. Dramatically placed blue-black exhaust stacks outside one of the buildings provide a memorable element of sculptural contrast.

Walter Gropius and the seven other members of The Architects Collaborative have produced in the Harvard Graduate Center a complex of buildings interesting for their version of

the courts and yards around which many of Harvard's older
school buildings are grouped. The brick and concrete cafeteria
and dormitory units of the Graduate Center are perhaps
lacking in the sensitive detail which makes Bulfinch's University
Hall and Richardson's Sever Hall so appealing, and their
proportions and structural details fail of being especially warm
or intimate or humanized no matter how studiously the buildings are sited at picturesque angles.

A ramp in the Center's main building has for a backdrop
a patterned tile wall designed by Herbert Bayer. Josef Albers
executed an abstract brick bas-relief, and fronting one of the
buildings is a tall, tree-like steel construction by Richard
Lippold.

Also in Cambridge, at 100 Memorial Drive, is the handsome
apartment house known as Eastgate. The building was designed
by Robert Kennedy, Karl Koch, Ralph Rapson, Vernon de
Mars, and William Brown. Eastgate's plan and elevations
depend on the use of skip-level corridors and elevator landings,
with duplex apartments on different floors entered from one
corridor; the apartments contain their own private stairs. The
complexity of this arrangement gives to the street facade its
alternating horizontal stripes of continuous windows (for the
corridors), and brick walls punctured with small windows (for
the apartments). On the side facing the Charles River the
building presents a colorful play of balconies large enough to
be useful—and nearly every apartment has one.

Marcel Breuer, who with Walter Gropius has already created
the basis of a contemporary idiom current in the north-eastern
states, has in his own work seldom produced a small house with
quite the élan of his cottage for Harry A. Caesar, in Lakeville,
Connecticut. Perched on a stone pedestal containing utility
rooms, the house is a wood box whose side walls project beyond
it like blinders, or like fences in mid-air. The living area,
considerably elevated, looks out on a lake. Two fascias connect
the wood blinders and frame the view, and between the fascias
and the glass wall of the living room there appears the top of a
tree. A massive concrete fireplace in the living room is placed
to cut directly into the view. The stone pedestal does not
entirely support the house: very thin wood columns are seen
at each side. They appear to be hanging from the bottom of
the house more than to be holding it up. One would suppose
that these columns are not necessarily meant to be seen, except
that just beneath the house they connect with exposed flat

Marcel Breuer, page 52

beams whose ends are covered with a pale gray board, in conspicuous contrast with the untreated wood used on the facade. A ramp leads up to the front door, and on this side of the house are elegant horizontal windows whose sliding glass sections are without frames. The effect of the whole building is subtle, deliberate and tense.

Perhaps the most strikingly mannered building of recent years is Alvar Aalto's dormitory for the Massachusetts Institute of Technology, in Cambridge. Spread out on Memorial Drive along the Charles River, the building presents a vast undulating facade of red brick. By planning it as a flattened W, Aalto was able to give most of the rooms a broad view of the river. Projecting from this curved facade is a small rectangular building containing the dining room; circular skylights, with spotlights held above them on metal stands, make this unit a kind of brightly lit stage for which the undulating red brick wall serves as a backdrop.

But on the north side, overlooking M.I.T. athletic fields, the same building is a jagged, angular composition, with strong diagonals cutting nervously across the facade. The effect is derived from a novel planning device: beginning at the ground floor, two continuous stairs cantilevered along the side of the building rise in opposite directions. Although they are enclosed, these two stairs seem tacked on to the outer wall like gigantic creeping vines. At each landing they leave behind them an ever larger space, given over chiefly to lounges and writing rooms. The upper part of the building, demarcated by the stairs, is surfaced in gray stone; the lower part is of red brick. The effect produced by the diagonal intersection of these two surfaces looks as though it was achieved by photomontage.

A desire to give each room the widest possible view of the river does not fully explain the building's complicated plan and bizarre contours. The justification, if not the appreciation, of these characteristics depends on their being clearly distinguished from the purposefully right-angled volumes with which most of today's multi-story buildings are planned. M.I.T.'s dormitory is a complex piece of sculpture, with an expressionist angularity which varies the forms modern architecture has already borrowed from cubist painting and sculpture, lending to these forms a new and perhaps overwrought emotional content.

Another successful departure from conventional form is Lloyd Wright's Wayfarers' Chapel in Palos Verdes, California. This building is a glass-enclosed redwood frame. Its triangular roof

Alvar Aalto, page 38

trusses are filled, alternately, with glass or copper. A refectory and a cloister are planned for the future, and giant redwood trees will ultimately surround the Chapel, arching over its glass roof in a pattern of sunlight and green shadow. Where Aalto's expressionism is massive and sculptural, Lloyd Wright's is linear and decorative, enclosing a volume with sharp outlines and angular planes of light. It may also be said that the emotional content of this building is suited to its purpose. The Wayfarers' Chapel is one of the very few modern buildings for religious celebrations that can be distinguished from a civic center or a gymnasium.

Lloyd Wright, page 124

The school buildings of Maynard Lyndon recall phases of Italian architecture in the 1920's and 1930's: stucco walls treated as though they were huge sheets of white cardboard (a technique early disparaged by Frank Lloyd Wright), the massing of connected units as if they were physically unconnected, and a general precision of detail valued for the illusion it creates of an architecture totally without detail. Lyndon contributes to this idiom a further refinement: wall and roof planes are projected beyond the facade, their leading edges often being fared down to a uniform and structurally improbable thinness. This detail suggests that the walls are not simply single pieces cut to size and assembled, but that end walls and roof are all cut and folded out of the same imaginary sheet of cardboard. Color is applied to enhance the effect.

The relative independence of Lyndon's architecture from the realities of structure is in contrast to its trimmed clarity and restraint, which we now habitually associate with an architecture reduced to its structural essentials. However, it may be argued that the skin, and not the bones beneath, is the decisive reality of a building. Stucco, the most uniform surface of all, is therefore used with structural logic if it unites the often discordant structural systems it covers.

Maynard Lyndon, page 80

The Miesian discipline, fixing its practitioners on the business of piecing together the elements of modern building, seems to have contributed to the success of the Case Study House designed by Charles Eames, for his own use, and built in California by the magazine *Arts and Architecture* as part of a continuing program already responsible for several distinguished buildings.

Put together with standard, factory produced elements, Eames' house is a two story metal cage. The walls are for the most part simply a collection of readily available steel windows and sliding doors. But the transparent web-like grid these units make is interrupted occasionally by solid panels of stucco, painted bright red, blue or white. A further enlivenment is produced by the limited use of translucent glass. Bedrooms are on a mezzanine floor opening onto a large, brightly lighted two story living room. Beneath the mezzanine is a low-ceilinged alcove with built-in seats and a fireplace.

Defining his problem as the enclosure of the maximum amount of space with the least expense, Eames resorted to materials and techniques which considerably accelerated construction. The alternately opaque, transparent, and translucent walls produce richly varied effects of scale; the steel frame itself is varied to include many small panels as well as single large sheets of plate glass, and the house unexpectedly draws out of industrial techniques a Japanese delicacy and decorativeness.

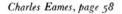
Charles Eames, page 58

Another excellent Case Study House built by *Arts and Architecture* illustrates an approach to problems of prefabrication and accelerated construction similar to that taken by Charles Eames, although it is an entirely different kind of house. Raphael Soriano has endeavored to develop a middle-ground procedure, realistically appraising available building techniques and organizing them to synthesize industrial and hand-crafted products with his particular concept of architectural space. The immediate result in Soriano's work is a variation of the basic disciplines of Mies and Le Corbusier's early buildings: a flat roof is supported by columns placed in regular bays; walls are independent screens freely placed. Interior partitions, however, Soriano has largely replaced by prefabricated closets. These storage walls are completely assembled in a cabinet-maker's shop, brought to the building after its roof is on, and then simply set in place. With much ingenuity Soriano has been able to produce the interior spaces of a house with little more than closets.

Raphael Soriano, page 108

Where Mies preserved a formal, classic balance in his treatment of walls and openings, Soriano has dispensed with any effort to unite the openings on a facade by their proportions and arrangement in relation to the length and height of the wall. The facades of his recent houses are organized instead by the rhythm of the structural bays, which tends to become repetitive and, internally, to force too great a similarity in room sizes. But Soriano has been able to offset these disadvantages with colorful materials (corrugated plastic and cork slabs for exterior walls) and with minor detail kept subordinate to the scale of the building.

Almost diametrically opposed to this rigidly organized kind of space is the glass house built by Philip Johnson in New Canaan, Connecticut. The house is a single room 32′ × 56′, with walls entirely of glass. There are no columns inside the house: all structural elements are part of the exterior wall, and the carefully articulated transitions from glass panel to steel column, as well as the subtle punctuation of space inside the house, constitute all its architecture. There is a single door in the center of each facade, establishing symmetrical axes for the whole house. Inside are low cabinets—one for kitchen equipment and another for storage—and a brick cylinder containing a bathroom and, on its outer wall, a fireplace. The exact placement of cabinets, brick cylinder, and a large piece of sculpture creates "rooms". The cabinets are of walnut and the cylinder,

Philip C. Johnson, page 72

35

Philip C. Johnson. page 72

like the floor of the house, is of red brick heavily waxed to bring out its color.

More painterly and flexible in its spatial organization than the glass house designed by Mies for Dr. Edith Farnsworth, the Johnson house, set on a flat shelf of lawn overlooking a wooded valley, calls to mind an eighteenth-century pavilion of classical proportions and romantic mood. With various elements asymmetrically grouped around symmetrical axes, its interior is a sequence of spaces organized with classical concern for beginning, middle, and end. In this respect it differs from much contemporary architecture.

Our buildings often lack the single dominating space which would justify their having been built. One reason for this is a prevalent indifference to just those refinements of sequence and proportion which have, after all, been fundamental to the art of architecture for several centuries. No doubt this indifference is due, in part, to an excessive preoccupation with what is merely functional. But another reason is that space is expensive to enclose, and clients are often obliged to fill up and render opaque what little they can afford.

Besides the houses by Eames and Soriano, and the amusing glass and aluminum dome in the Arizona desert by Paolo Soleri and Mark Mills, there have been in recent years two particularly striking efforts to organize space by methods which, however, are not immediately applicable to all building programs. The corn refining plant at Corpus Christi, Texas, designed by Frank R. Whitney of the H. K. Ferguson Company, was the solution to a highly specialized industrial problem. The buildings are concrete cages in which machines are freely arranged like books on a shelf. Whitney discarded not only windows but entire walls, thus arriving at buildings almost entirely open to the weather—an arrangement appropriate both to the particular processes involved and to the warm Texas climate. In its integration of complex activities within a single framework, the factory resembles an early sketch by Le Corbusier for a United Nations building on a site in Connecticut. In this design Le Corbusier took each department of the organization and separately packaged it, installing them all in one vast concrete cage. A similar articulation of functions might produce houses with prefabricated rooms like the single pieces of furniture we now buy in stores. These units would be casually arranged in a light, demountable framework.

A more radical approach to the problem of shelter design is that suggested by Buckminster Fuller. By fractionizing the surface of a sphere into almost equilateral triangles, Fuller is able to design domes of theoretically unlimited dimensions. Experimental domes of aluminum tubes have been built in the United States and in Canada. In its ideal version a dome for residential use would be sheathed with translucent and transparent plastic, and fitted inside with a curtain like a folding fan. All living areas would be sheltered underneath the dome, but only part of the ground area need be paved. Most of it could be used for gardens and a pool. Areas requiring privacy would be pavilions built of light, soundproof materials, and the "house" would be equipped with portable mechanical packages for heat and water supply. The general living space thus becomes a high-ceilinged garden—the ceiling itself being a transparent umbrella reaching to the ground.

Fuller's Geodesic Dome is the product of complex analytical thought and an intuitive perception of the aesthetics possible for a technological society. Architecture would thus begin with man's control of the earth itself, and total mechanization, in Fuller's view, would enable us to return to our earliest recorded home: the Garden of Eden.

Buckminster Fuller

Buckminster Fuller

Alvar Aalto

Perry, Shaw, and Hepburn, associated

SENIOR DORMITORY FOR

MASSACHUSETTS INSTITUTE OF TECHNOLOGY

Cambridge, Massachusetts. 1948

The building was made serpentine in plan to
give all rooms a broad view of the Charles
River; the undulating red brick facade serves as
a backdrop for the small dining room. Stairs
climbing up the side of the building leave extra
space behind them, on each floor, for a lounge.

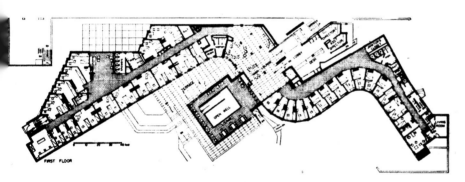

FIRST FLOOR

Richard L. Aeck and Associates

FOOTBALL STADIUM FOR

·HENRY GRADY HIGH SCHOOL

Atlanta, Georgia. 1948

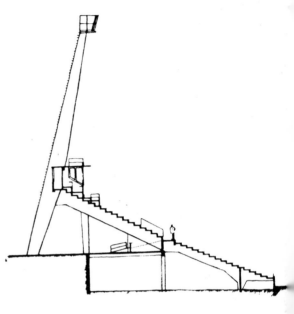

These reinforced concrete grandstands seat 10,000 spectators. The field is used by six city high schools for about 50 football games and track meets a year; night games are the rule. Tapering structural light standards (the bottom 40′ are working supports) hold floodlights 102′ above the field. Each stand is entered by four ramps opening onto a central cross aisle feeding six vertical aisles.

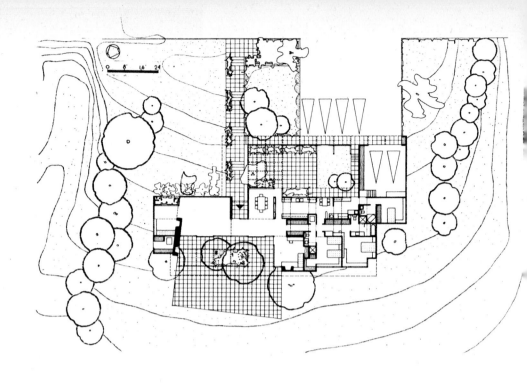

Gregory Ain

Joseph Johnson, Alfred Day, associated

HOUSE FOR JOHN WILFONG

Los Angeles, California. 1952

The two living rooms and the dining room of this house may all be closed off from a central hall by large sliding walls. The house is set on a sloping site, with a broad terrace and planted area raised above ground level. The dining room opens on to a walled patio. Materials are redwood and stucco.

Edward Larrabee Barnes HOUSE FOR TED WEINER *Fort Worth, Texas.* 1952

In addition to its living and dining rooms, the large game room of this house opens on a marble-paved covered terrace. The main entrance, through a walled garden, is partially roofed with a trellis of translucent plastic.

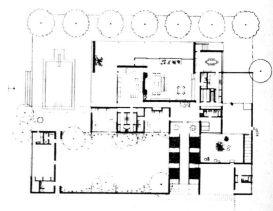

Donald Barthelme and Associates

WEST COLUMBIA ELEMENTARY SCHOOL

West Columbia, Texas. 1952

Structural details of the steel frame used in this school have been exposed for their decorative value, with particular effectiveness in the playground patio. Top-lighted louvered ceilings in all the classrooms balance the light from glass walls and eliminate glare. Children are delivered to the school in buses; the vaulted concrete canopy fronting the building provides shelter along the driveway.

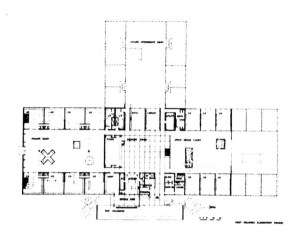

Pietro Belluschi

OFFICE BUILDING FOR

EQUITABLE SAVINGS AND LOAN ASSOCIATION

Portland, Oregon. 1948

Glass and aluminum sheathing on this twelve story concrete frame produces a smooth, sparkling facade. No part projects more than seven-eighths of an inch.

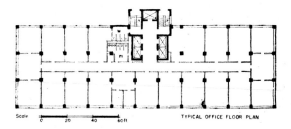

TYPICAL OFFICE FLOOR PLAN

Scale 0 20 40 60 ft

Marcel Breuer

DORMITORY FOR VASSAR COLLEGE

Poughkeepsie, New York. 1951

Girls living in Vassar's Cooperative Dormitory do their own housework, including cooking. Kitchen, dining room and lounge are in a one story pavilion attached to the main building by a glass-walled lobby. Bedrooms are on the second floor; a projecting sunshade of corrugated asbestos board overhangs their windows.

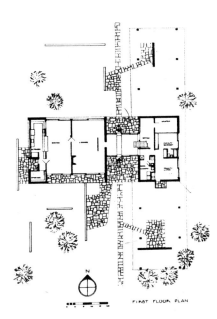

FIRST FLOOR PLAN

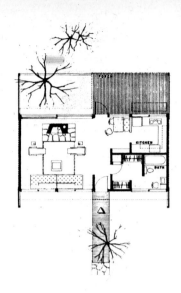

Marcel Breuer

HOUSE FOR HARRY A. CAESAR

Lakeville, Connecticut. 1952

A stone pedestal (housing utility and storage rooms) supports a wood box containing living areas, kitchen, and bath. Access to the upper level is by a wood ramp. Cantilevered beams at the narrow ends of the house have diagonal cypress siding bolted to them, thus extending in mid-air fences designed to frame the view and insure privacy.

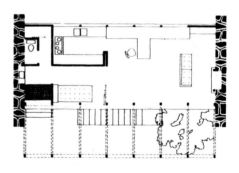

In a climate offering heavy winter rains and extreme summer heat, with a variety of insects, the architect has suspended the upper living area of this house between two walls of fieldstone and one of screening. The living area can be closed to the weather by sliding glass panels; plastic screening stretched on wood frames over and around this facade protects the interior from insects and increases the apparent size of the house.

Mario Corbett HOUSE FOR MORITZ THOMSEN *Vina, California.* 1952

Gardner A. Dailey and Associates

Walter T. Steilberg, associated

RED CROSS HEADQUARTERS

San Francisco, California. 1948

Gray concrete walls were poured in V-jointed tongue and groove boards, set vertically, to produce a finely ribbed surface texture. Interior offices open on a central court; on the top floor, adjoining a sundeck, there is an auditorium which is also used as an employees' cafeteria.

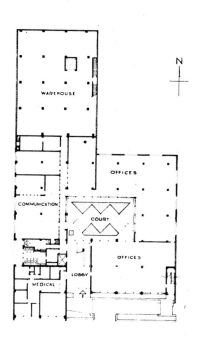

Charles Eames CASE STUDY HOUSE *Santa Monica, California.* 1949

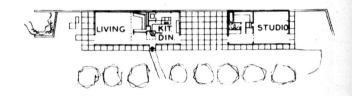

Factory produced steel window and door units, as well as steel framing and roof decking, accelerated construction of this house. The metal frames are filled with transparent or translucent glass and panels of stucco painted with primary colors or white. The main part of the living area is two stories high. Bedrooms are on a mezzanine floor which opens into the living room; beneath the mezzanine is a small alcove with built-in seats and bookcases.

H. K. Ferguson Company

Frank L. Whitney, project architect

BLUEBONNET PLANT, CORN PRODUCTS REFINING CO.

Corpus Christi, Texas. 1949

The Bluebonnet plant for the processing of corn products occupies 140 acres. At each phase of its design the architects re-examined the manufacturing process itself. In this way it was determined that many processes customarily enclosed in weatherproof buildings need not be enclosed at all, particularly in the Gulf climate. The architects accordingly left out not only the windows but the walls as well. The Mill House (left) and the Steep House (right) ultimately became extensions of the machinery itself—platforms, a roof, and some sunshades.

Walter Gropius and The Architects Collaborative

HARVARD GRADUATE CENTER

Cambridge, Massachusetts. 1950

Harvard's new Graduate Center has eight buildings arranged to enclose a series of large and small quadrangles. No building is more than four stories high; construction is of concrete with exterior walls of buff-colored brick or limestone. The members of The Architects Collaborative are Jean Bodman-Fletcher, Norman C. Fletcher, John C. Harkness, Sarah Harkness, Robert S. McMillan, Louis A. McMillen, and Benjamin Thompson.

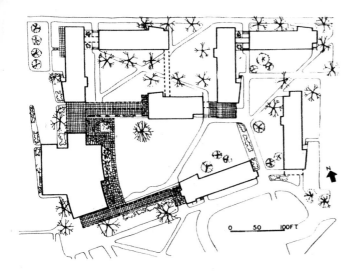

63

Harwell Hamilton Harris

HOUSE FOR RALPH JOHNSON

Los Angeles, California. 1951

Built on a steep suburban lot, the three levels of this house form steps up the hillside. The roof of the garage serves as a terrace for the second floor apartment; major living areas are at the top, with a dining room and patio at the rear. The entire building is planned on a 3′ module. All framing members are exposed.

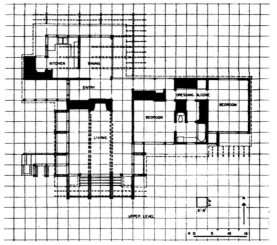

65

Harrison and Abramovitz

Mitchell & Ritchey and Altenhof & Brown, associated

ALCOA BUILDING

Pittsburgh, Pennsylvania. 1952

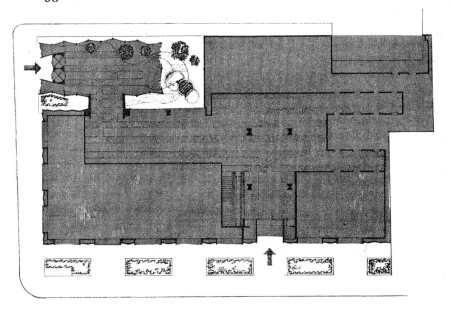

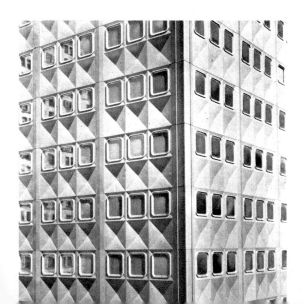

Built by the Aluminum Company of America for
its own use, this 30 story tower is sheathed with
6′ × 12′ prefabricated aluminum sheet panels.
Windows, built into the panels, are reversible
and have heat- and glare-treated glass. The
entrance hall, four and a half stories high, is
a separate, glass-walled structure whose roof is
cantilevered from the main tower.

Wallace K. Harrison
and consultants

UNITED NATIONS SECRETARIAT

New York, New York. 1950

Providing office accommodation for 3,400 employees, the Secretariat is a 39 story building with an aluminum grille to conceal equipment on the roof. The narrow end walls are of white marble; the other two elevations are surfaced with green-tinted glass. Floors devoted to mechanical equipment divide these glass facades into three parts. Wallace K. Harrison was Director of Planning; Max Abramovitz, Deputy Director of Planning. The Board of Design Consultants were G. A. Soilleux, Australia; Gaston Brunfaut, Belgium; Oscar Niemeyer, Brazil; Ernest Cormier, Canada; Ssu-Ch'eng Liang, China; Charles Le Corbusier, France; Sven Markelius, Sweden; N. D. Bassov, Union of Soviet Socialist Republics; Howard Robertson, United Kingdom; Julio Vilamajo, Uruguay.

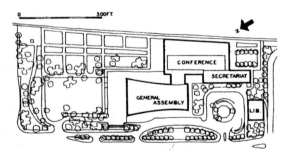

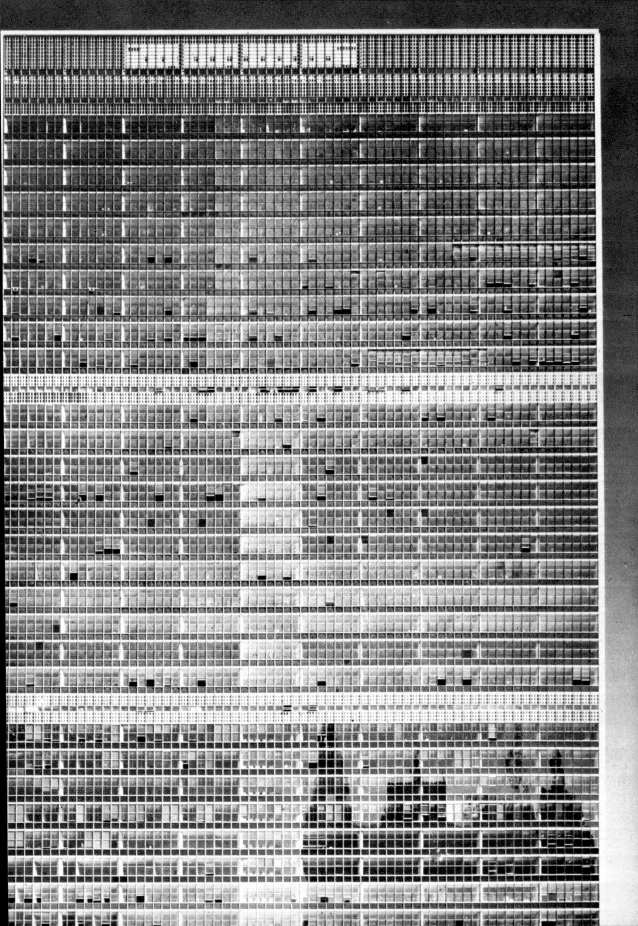

John MacL. Johansen

HOUSE FOR JOHN MACL. JOHANSEN

New Canaan, Connecticut. 1949

On the top floor are living, study, and service
areas, the first two being separated by a fireplace
built into a low cabinet. A moderately sloping
site allows bedrooms to be placed on a lower level,
partially below grade, with window-sills a few
inches above the lawn.

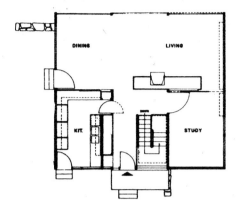

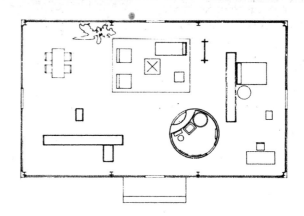

Philip C. Johnson

HOUSE FOR PHILIP C. JOHNSON

New Canaan, Connecticut. 1949

The completely open glass and steel house is the major element of an architectural composition which includes outdoor sculpture and a separate blank-walled brick guest house. Spatial divisions in the glass building are achieved by a brick cylinder containing a bathroom, and by low walnut cabinets—one of them containing kitchen equipment. The red brick floor and cylinder are waxed to bring out a cold purple overtone. The steel is painted dark gray; steps and a railing are of white granite.

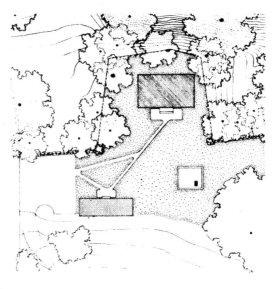

73

Philip C. Johnson

Landis Gores, associated

HOUSE FOR RICHARD HODGSON

New Canaan, Connecticut. 1951

Except in the combined dining and entrance hall, and in one wall in the living room, major glass walls in this house open on a heavily planted patio. There are three bedrooms, and the plan provides for access to a projected bedroom wing. The floor is of dark gray tile; walls are white plaster or pale gray glazed brick.

Apartments in this building on the Charles River are entered from a corridor on every third floor. Tenants living above or below corridor floors have vestibules and a private stair up or down. The skip-floor elevator arrangement, by reducing corridor space, allows through ventilation to apartments on two out of three floors. Living rooms have glass walls and large balconies; services include a garage, and a community room on the roof.

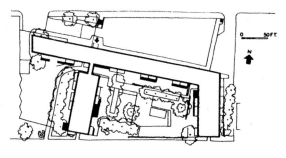

Kennedy, Koch, DeMars, Rapson and Brown

APARTMENT HOUSE AT 100 MEMORIAL DRIVE

Cambridge, Massachusetts. 1950

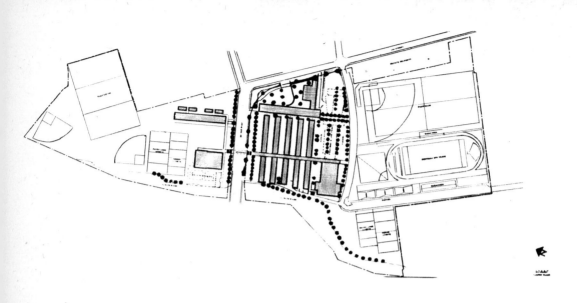

Ernest J. Kump

SAN JOSE HIGH SCHOOL

San Jose, California. 1952

Some of the numerous buildings in this vast
school project are reached by a tunnel under the
road dividing the site. Of concrete frame construction, the buildings have glass walls for each
of the classrooms. A separate cafeteria building
also serves as a community center.

ynard Lyndon

A ELEMENTARY SCHOOL

ı, California. 1950

rooms in these one story units are entered
a covered walk which connects all the
ings. A clerestory window above a louvered
g in each classroom provides back-lighting;
najor light source, in each room, is a glass
Exterior stucco walls are painted white
occasional color accents; landscaping is in-
lete.

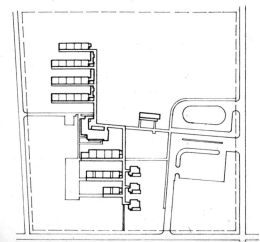

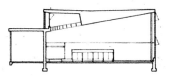

82

Eric Mendelsohn

MAIMONIDES HEALTH CENTER

San Francisco, California. 1950

Most of the rooms for the 87 patients in this concrete and glass hospital face south and have access to cantilevered balconies overlooking a landscaped court. White iron railings leave the view unobstructed, and projecting columns screen the glass-walled rooms from each other.

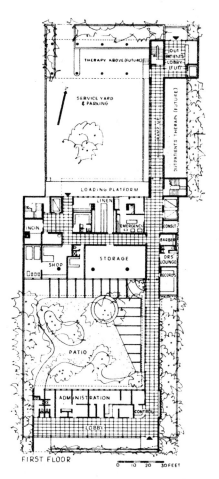

FIRST FLOOR

0   10   20   30 FEET

Ludwig Mies van der Rohe

HOUSE FOR DR. EDITH FARNSWORTH

Plano, Illinois. 1950

The house consists of floor and roof planes suspended between 8 steel columns, to which their steel channel fascias are welded. A broad platform, set lower and to one side of the house, is also held above the ground between steel posts. Exterior walls are of glass; a wood-panelled utility core at one side of the room contains kitchen, bathrooms, heating unit, and fireplace. The steel frame was sandblasted and painted white; the steps and all floors are of Italian travertine.

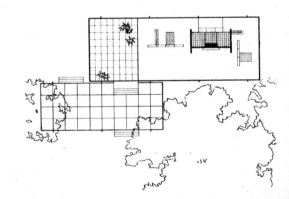

Ludwig Mies van der Rohe

Pace Associates and Holsman, Holsman, Klekamp and Taylor, associated

APARTMENT HOUSES

AT 860 LAKE SHORE DRIVE

Chicago, Illinois. 1951

These two buildings, identical in size, overlook Lake Michigan. Exterior walls are entirely of glass. Both buildings are steel-clad concrete frames 26 stories high. Steel I-beams applied to the facades serve as window mullions and make decorative vertical stripes, changing in density according to the angle at which the buildings are viewed. To keep the glass facades uniform in color, all apartments are equipped with gray curtains (instead of venetian blinds). Tenants may install their own curtains behind those provided with the apartments. There is an underground garage, and the two buildings are connected by a covered walk. All steel is painted black; window frames are aluminum. The buildings stand on a travertine platform.

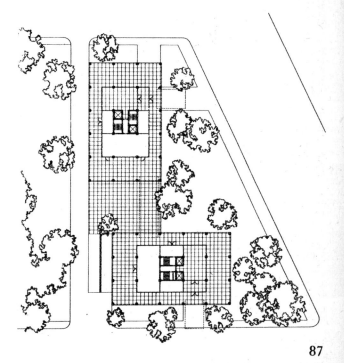

Ludwig Mies van der Rohe

Sargent and Lundy, and Frank J.
Kornacker, consultants

BOILER PLANT,

ILLINOIS INSTITUTE OF TECHNOLOGY

Chicago, Illinois. 1950

Similar in detail to the school buildings designed
by Mies for the Illinois Institute of Technology,
this boiler plant is a steel frame filled with
buff-colored brick panels on its major elevations.

Richard J. Neutra

HOUSE FOR WARREN TREMAINE

Montecito, California. 1949

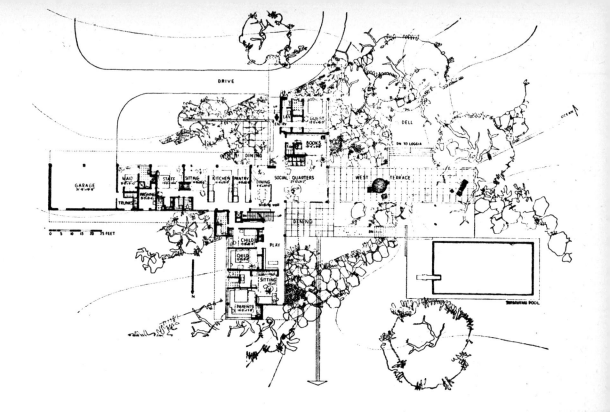

A living-dining area is placed at the center of a plan resembling a pinwheel; bedrooms, services and pool pavilion are each in separate radiating wings. The roof is a thin slab resting on heavy posts and beams of reinforced concrete, sand-blasted or painted white. Masonry walls are of buff-colored sandstone.

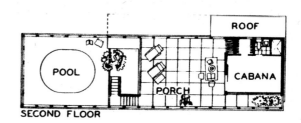

SECOND FLOOR

Igor Polevitsky

HOUSE FOR MICHAEL HELLER

Miami, Florida. 1949

Concrete block walls painted pale blue support a wood and steel frame enclosed with plastic screening: two-thirds of the house is open to the weather. An oval swimming pool above ground level and a Bucida tree are enclosed by the screen walls and roof.

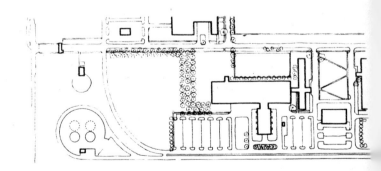

Saarinen, Saarinen and Associates

Smith, Hinchman and Grylls, Inc., associated

GENERAL MOTORS TECHNICAL CENTER

Detroit, Michigan. 1951

Constructed of steel frames filled with brick or glass, these three buildings are the first to be completed for General Motors Technical Center. The glazed ceramic sand-molded brick is used in varying tones of burnt orange and bright blue. The office building, adjoining a rectangular pool, has no movable windows: the heat absorbing green-tinted glass, set in matte-gray enamel frames, is permanently fixed. Air conditioning and lighting fixtures are incorporated in the grid pattern of the ceilings. The dramatic rows of blue-black stacks on either side of the dynamometer building (next two pages) are used to exhaust engine gases.

Saarinen, Saarinen and Associates

Smith, Hinchman and Grylls, Inc., associated

GENERAL MOTORS TECHNICAL CENTER

Detroit, Michigan. 1951

Saarinen, Swanson and Saarinen

OPERA SHED FOR BERKSHIRE MUSIC CENTER

Stockbridge, Massachusetts. 1947

The opera shed accommodates the Berkshire Music Center's productions of small operas and orchestral concerts. An auditorium of the required volume was achieved by exposing, above the roof, a series of trusses with laminated wood arch upper chords. The stepped-down roof itself lies in the planes of the bottom chords of the trusses (which also serve as girders) and provides equal distribution of sound waves.

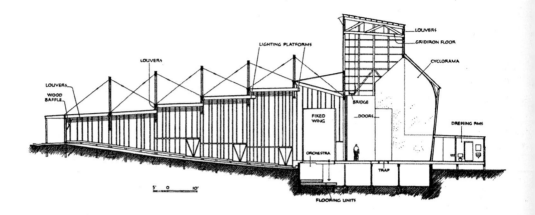

LOUVERS

GRIDIRON FLOOR

LIGHTING PLATFORMS

CYCLORAMA

LOUVERS

LOUVERS

WOOD
BAFFLE

BRIDGE

FIXED
WING

DOORS

DRESSING RMS.

ORCHESTRA

TRAP

5' 0   10'

FLOORING UNITS

Schweikher and Elting

HOUSE FOR LOUIS C. UPTON

Paradise Valley, Arizona. 1950

Four separate units—a living and service area, master's suite, guest house, and servant's quarters—are grouped under a single roof providing covered outdoor alcoves. All living areas open on a cactus garden and a pool (with a fireplace projecting into it) which borders the living room. Masonry walls are of concrete poured around desert stone. The trellised sundeck on the roof is enclosed by copper screening.

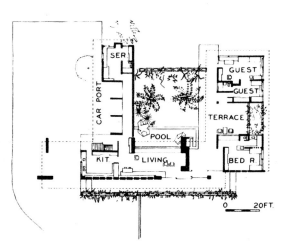

Skidmore, Owings and Merrill

Gordon Bunschaft, chief designer

LEVER HOUSE

New York City, New York. 1952

The only enclosed areas on the ground floor of this office building for Lever Brothers are reception and display rooms. The remaining space, designed for the citizens of New York, is given over to pedestrian walks and a garden. An employees' cafeteria on the third floor, with its paved and landscaped roof terrace, is visible from adjoining buildings. The 24 story tower, occupying considerably less of its site than is allowed by law, is sheathed in stainless steel and blue-green heat resistant glass (1404 panes). Windows are cleaned from a traveling gondola suspended from the roof.

Skidmore, Owings and Merrill

GARDEN APARTMENTS

Oak Ridge, Tennessee. 1950

Of the 415 housing units in this project, 24 are one-bedroom apartments; the remainder have two bedrooms. An excellent plan provides most of the living rooms with screened balconies, and kitchens are accessible from a service porch. Landscaping is incomplete.

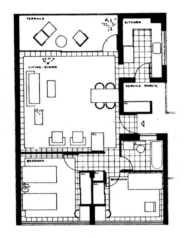

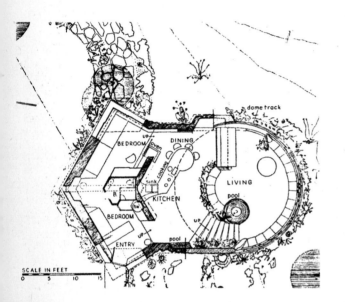

SCALE IN FEET
0   5   10   15

Paolo Soleri and Mark Mills

DESERT HOUSE

Cave Creek, Arizona. 1951

A glass and aluminum dome covers the main living space; sleeping and service areas are within the stone podium, dug into the hillside. Built of half sections which may be rotated inside one another, the outer section of the dome is aluminum-painted for protection from the sun. A copper tube at the perimeter sprays a cooling curtain of water, and a concrete ramp beneath the stair carries water from the living room pool to exterior planting.

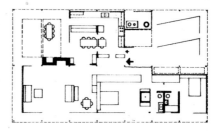

Raphael Soriano

CASE STUDY HOUSE FOR

ARTS AND ARCHITECTURE

Los Angeles, California. 1950

Columns are painted dark blue, fascia and exposed framing bright red; the translucent corrugated plastic is pale yellow. Steel columns in 10′ × 20′ bays support the flat roof, and the arrangement of rooms is determined by the placement of prefabricated storage wall units which serve as interior partitions.

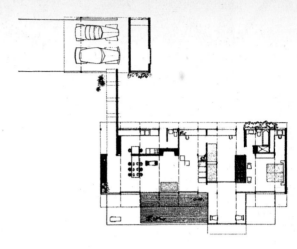

Twitchell and Rudolph

HOUSE FOR ALBERT SIEGRIST

Venice, Florida. 1949

A cypress frame is filled with lime blocks and plate glass; the 10 structural bents, visible inside the house, are joined on the south side by a continuous wood tie, which also conceals tracks for the sliding glass walls. Major rooms are on the south, overlooking a reflecting pool. The screened porch is partially roofed with glass.

Twitchell and Rudolph

HOUSE FOR W. R. HEALY

Sarasota, Florida. 1950

This pavilion at the edge of a Florida bayou
combines post and lintel wood construction with
a roof of weathertight plastic that can move and
stretch. It is made of steel flat bars suspended in
their catenary curve, supporting fiber boards
and flexible insulation sprayed top and bottom
with "cocoon" (a vinyl plastic used by the Navy
to protect equipment in storage). North and
south walls are of glass; east and west elevations
are filled with wood jalousies for sun control.

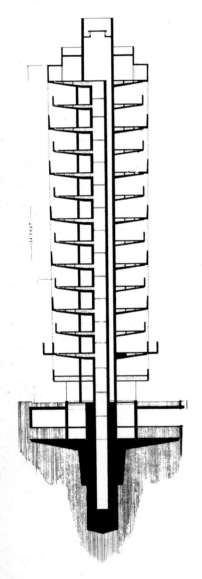

Frank Lloyd Wright

LABORATORY FOR JOHNSON WAX COMPANY

Racine, Wisconsin. 1949

Alternating square and circular floors are cantilevered from a central shaft containing an elevator, stairs, and plumbing. Each laboratory has a circular mezzanine floor. The two story high exterior walls are made of horizontal translucent glass tubing. Except for its structural core, the whole tower stands free of the ground and is set in a walled courtyard.

Frank Lloyd Wright

STORE FOR V. C. MORRIS

San Francisco, California. 1949

On San Francisco's Maiden Lane passers-by discover a windowless buff-colored brick wall with a single arched opening cut into it. Walking through this into a tunnel with a vaulted roof half brick, half glass, their gaze is directed to a ramp ascending, in a great curve, toward a luminous ceiling of plastic plates and bubbles. China, glass, and silver are displayed in walnut showcases and circular niches. A tray filled with plants is suspended by piano wires in the space enclosed by the ramp. Colors are cream, beige, black and gold

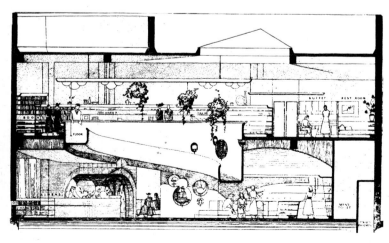

Frank Lloyd Wright

HOUSE FOR HERBERT JACOBS

Middleton, Wisconsin. 1948

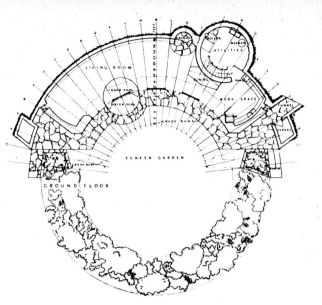

The Jacobs house, on a wind-swept plain, is a two story hemicycle protected on the north by an earth bank. All rooms open to a sunken garden on the south. Bedrooms, overlooking the garden, are on a mezzanine floor set back from the glass doors, so that from within the volume of the house registers as one large room with minor subdivisions. A tunnel through the earth bank leads directly into the garden—the site itself being used as an architectural material.

Frank Lloyd Wright

HOUSE FOR SOL FRIEDMAN

Pleasantville, New York. 1949

In plan the house is developed from two intersecting circles, one for the main living area, the other, higher up, for the service area. Bedrooms are on a second floor which opens as a balcony into the two story high living room. The sloping masonry walls of the living area have crenelated windows. Circular roofs on the house and on the carport are of wood and concrete.

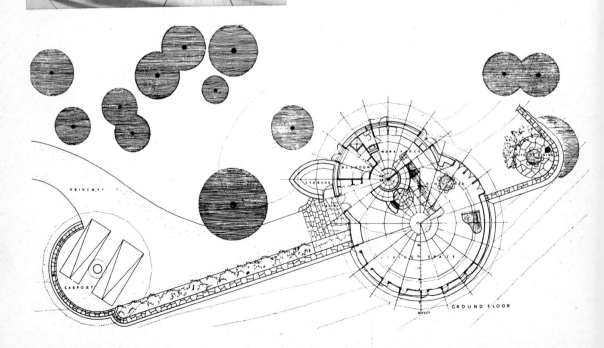

Lloyd Wright

WAYFARERS' CHAPEL

Palos Verdes, California. 1951

Designed as a place of worship for the followers of theologian Emanuel Swedenborg, the chapel and its newly planted grove are the first stage of a project which will include a carillon tower, a community house, and a cloister. The chapel is built of redwood frames dividing its roof into alternating panels of glass and pale blue tile. The transparent, web-like elevations are intended to be only partially visible; a grove of redwood trees will ultimately enclose the building in a giant natural arch of shadow.

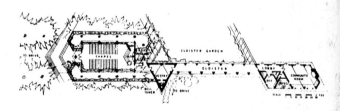

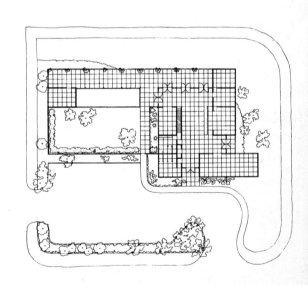

John Yeon

VISITORS' INFORMATION CENTER

Portland, Oregon. 1949

The Visitors' Information Center was commissioned by the Chamber of Commerce and public authorities. Four rectangular units of varying height contain staff offices, exhibition areas, rest rooms, and garden equipment—the latter being placed at the end of a long pool bordered by a pergola. Exterior walls are of plywood panels painted dark blue-green, the exposed framing members are painted blue-black, trim is pale green, and doors are dark red.

This book has been produced in December 1952 for the
Trustees of the Museum of Modern Art by Thames & Hudson
Ltd., London. Printed by Jarrold & Sons Ltd., Norwich,
England.